The American Dream Lost

T R CHATHAM

ISBN: 1470012626
ISBN-13: 978-1470012625

DEDICATION

To the founders who launched this great experiment in freedom.

CONTENTS

INTRODUCTION

The socioeconomic model that the United States has used and benefited from since its conception is failing. It is not a failure of capitalism or free markets but of people and ideologies. The great tribulation we face as a nation will produce winners and losers to create the next chapter of our history. Many still refuse to believe what is happening or are willing to adjust to their new reality. This book will act as a primer to stimulate your creativity and ingenuity and allow you to build a raft to safely navigate the flood waters and reach a safe harbor with a minimum of pain and suffering. If you act in time you will be able to maintain a reasonable standard of living and build a new and productive life. How soon you act and the steps you take will determine what your future will look like. Forces are now building that will devastate most people financially and spiritually. Only those that heed the warnings of history will be able to shelter themselves and emerge strong enough to move forward in a productive way. Your future is up to you.

1
American Dreaming

What is the American dream? What makes it American versus Russian or Chinese? The one thing that has set America apart from all others over the years is the freedom we have had to invent and develop ideas. This country was founded on ideas the likes of which had never been conceived before. A man should be free to live his life as he pleases and do as he wants as long as it does not hurt others was a new idea. It was an idea that appealed to many. So strongly did they feel about this that they left their homes and set out across a dangerous ocean not knowing if they would make it to this land where the laws of men did not yet exist. With only their trust in God and each other and the ideas they dreamed of, they created the most prosperous nation in the history of the world. They were not prosperous because of new cities that had been built for them, or crops that had been planted for them, or new machines that had been invented for them. They came to an empty land with vast natural untapped resources. The freedom they enjoyed allowed them to build their own cities, plant their own crops and invent incredible new machines. The natural resources were important but it was their freedom that allowed their growth, prosperity and inventiveness. Freedom allowed them to be as much as they could dream to be. Without really knowing or understanding exactly what it is, people have espoused about living the American dream. The American dream to some is being prosperous in a monetary way. To some it is following their dreams and doing something that they enjoy doing regardless of wealth. In the end the American dream in its purist sense is about the unrestricted freedom to do what makes us happy. That is what set us apart from all other countries. That is what produced our prosperity and happiness.

The dream is fading along with our happiness and prosperity. The American dream has been hijacked by the same evils that have perverted and destroyed it the world over since the beginning of time. It is being ruled and regulated and taxed away by those who have different dreams. Their dreams of wealth and control know no ends. If it is allowed to continue the dream that is unrestricted freedom will die and people will suffer the misery of its progeny, totalitarianism. Not understanding that the dream is actually the availability of freedom, many will let it slip away like grains of sand through their fingers until one day nothing is left. Rome was not built in a day. It was built brick by brick over many years just as freedom and prosperity are. All too easily it can be destroyed little by little without much notice until the day people realize it no longer exists. When nations die they end much like cloudy days, with no discernable sunset, no specific moment between light and darkness, just a dim glow that fades into obscurity until nothing remains. The more something degrades the harder it becomes to restore it. Once it is completely destroyed it must be rebuilt from scratch which is a long and difficult process. The American dream is dying and people are at a loss to understand why. They think if they emulate other countries or philosophies they will regain it but this only carries them further away from the dream. Until they rediscover that freedom is the key to happiness and prosperity the slide into the abyss will continue. If the lessons of the past have to be relearned then it will be a long and difficult journey for this nation and its people. History has also taught us that every fiat currency ever created has collapsed. Fiat currency is a confidence game that turns all of its users into debt slaves before ultimately destroying them. The United States is no different than any other country and our time is rapidly approaching. When currencies begin to die governments tighten their control on the people to maintain their power and wealth. When paper money dies you can be sure that those in power have already converted their wealth into tangible items such as gold, property and factories that produce goods. They know that only tangible items are real wealth. The people need to follow this example and do the same before it's too late. The governments prolific spending is increasing at an alarming rate. We are now at the point that to stop this spending will cause a great deal of pain for the people but continued spending will eventually end the same way and the pain will be unbearable. To put it simply, we can amputate a toe now or the whole leg later. Which would you prefer? One of the things people equate to the American dream is our standard of living. The abundance that has been created from our freedom over the years is emulated by many across the world. There is little you cannot do or find in America. Most in this country who have never traveled abroad do not understand the incredible gift we have inherited from our forefathers. It is this lack of understanding that has led to deterioration of our country and our values. Few who enjoy freedom realize the suffering and sacrifice that was necessary to gain it or is required to maintain it. Few are willing to make the sacrifice, instead opting to ride the gravy train never understanding that this ride ends at the bottom of a cliff. The American dream is dying and the only way to save it is to reexamine the way we are living and recapture the spirit that made us great. Nothing in life is free and the cost to regain freedom lost will exact a high cost in blood, sweat and tears. One of the great benefits of our freedom has been our standard of living. It has been decaying for many years because of fraud, waste and abuse in a system that has been perverted to benefit the few while taking from the many. We need to reexamine the way we live and get back to basics in order to regain what we have lost. We need to get back to a business model that has been proven to work. We need to regain a level of freedom and a standard of living that we are losing. To build anything you must start with a good foundation and work up from there. A lot of the decay in our society can be attributed to the decline in our moral underpinnings. When people loose respect for the private property rights of others and accept graft and corruption as a normal part of doing business, the destruction of wealth and prosperity will soon follow. Real wealth is difficult to build and very easy to destroy as many are now finding out. Only through hard work and honest business practices can a nation prosper and grow. That is not to deny that a few corrupt individuals can and have in fact attained unimaginable wealth in this nation. But these individuals have done so at the cost of many others and this wealth is not beneficial to the greater population but in fact hinders the honest business economy and prevents the upward mobility of those affected. One of the mechanisms that has accomplished this is the lobbying efforts of big business that has caused higher taxes, rules and regulations that have forced many small businesses to close and other companies to move overseas. Those that have lost good paying manufacturing jobs to outsourcing now have to make do with lower paying jobs with less upward mobility. This causes these people to have a lower standard of living which flows through the economy causing others to have a lower living standard. A lot of wealth and productive capability can be retroactively destroyed because people who otherwise might have brought new ideas and products to market are dissuaded from doing so due to the smaller slower economy. Many will try to defend this outsourcing as a good thing but it ultimately makes everyone a lot poorer in the affected country. If left unchecked, this can destroy a country and its production capability. This can lead to people having to live in a third world economy when they don't have to. This is a reality that we are beginning to experience in the U.S. as time passes. Your standard of living is relative. It is made up of all of the things that are available to you that enhance your quality of life and happiness. Everyone has their own idea of happiness so the standard of living will be different for everyone. A man living on a mountain top in a cabin with no running water and no electricity might be very satisfied with his life. If he has shelter, food, clothing and a caring family that might be everything he wants from life. The more you want, the more you will have to labor and earn. For some, having lots of things will mean happiness, for others just having a family to come home to every night will fulfill their needs and wants. A standard of living and happiness are two distinctly different things but they go hand in hand to complement each other. A standard of living involves tangible things that make life easier while happiness is for the most part a state of mind. So don't confuse your standard of living with your happiness. Most people don't understand the relationship between these two things and their lives are always out of balance because of it. Having tangible things will increase your productive capability but they won't make you happy in and of themselves. Your happiness comes from feeling a sense of accomplishment and belonging in the actions that you take. Knowing what makes you happy and what you want out of life is the first step to achieving it. A high standard of living is just icing on the cake, not the cake itself. So, don't confuse yourself.

2
Live Free and Prosper

A core element of freedom is being independent in business and in life. Business independence in most cases means being self employed. Being self employed places your destiny mostly in your control. You determine what product to sell, how much to sell it for, the best way to produce it, how to market it and how many hours you are willing to invest in it. The more time and energy you invest in it the greater your profit potential. This is the ethic that built America into an industrial giant. Unfortunately today many, that lack the drive to work hard and lack the imagination to produce something new, harbor great resentment for those that do. Instead of working to produce value in the economy these people seek to tear down and appropriate the fruits of success of the successful. They abhor those that are rich, even though many of those people earned it through sweat and perseverance. They don't think it's fair for others to have more than they do. They feel it's only right for the successful in society to give them their share because they feel they deserve it. Unrestricted freedom provides equal opportunity to succeed as well as to fail. If you fail in your quest for prosperity, it is because of a failing of your own and no one else's. Equal opportunity does not guarantee equal success. Those that seek an equal outcome are the cause of a rot in society that ultimately destroys freedom for all. In your quest to be a successful businessman you need to keep a low profile and avoid these people at all cost. They will be detrimental to your freedom and your prosperity and will not hesitate to single you out for all of their failings in life. A key to financial success is to be prosperous while maintaining the appearance of being average. Live within your means and store your excess wealth in a form that cannot be inflated away or easily stolen from you. This may mean storing some of your wealth in consumer goods and commodities that you will need at a later date. The greatest store of wealth that you can invest in is knowledge. As Ben Franklin once said "If a man pours his wallet into his head, no one can take it from him". Another storage device would be production equipment that you can use to produce a product to sell. This could be in the form of tools, machines or livestock. If you buy at today's prices, any increase in price inflation will be the same as earning that much in interest on the amount of money you spent. Some of the things you might want to store are clothing, household goods and related items, basic hygiene items, food items, home repair items and related hardware, auto parts and chemicals, fuel and energy related items and lawn and garden supplies. This type of storage plan will protect you from inflation as well as shortages if the supply system is disrupted in any way.

The best business is one that requires a minimum of equipment, is in great demand everywhere, and can be shut down during a slowdown and restarted with minimal time and expense. Some businesses that would fit this description would be a produce stand , flower stand , lawn maintenance , radiator repair , alternator or starter rebuilding , gun smithing , welding, metal fabrication/machining, auto repair, carpentry , plumbing , sewing , baking , barber shop/beauty salon , private instruction and upholstery repair. All of these require a minimum of equipment and space in relation to the income they can generate.

3
Inflation/Deflation/Hyperinflation

Let's clarify something that confuses many people. The amount of money in existence will always equal the value of all goods in existence. That is how we arrive at a price for everything we buy. The free market will do this price setting on its own. If the amount of goods in existence rises and the amount of money in existence stays the same, the price of goods will fall. The same amount of money divided by more goods equals' lower price per unit. If the amount of money in existence increases and the amount of goods stays the same, the price of goods will rise. More money divided by the same amount of goods equals' higher price per unit. When more money is released into the economy, the money supply is inflated, this results in the price of goods increasing and we call this inflation. When less money is available in the economy, the money supply is deflated, this causes the price of goods to fall and we call this deflation. If money is created and you get to use this money before it causes inflation it benefits you a great deal. Therefore, if you are first in line to get this new money you will like inflation. Bankers like inflation a lot because they get the new money first. If you have money saved inflation will decrease the amount of goods you will be able to buy with it so inflation is bad for you. If the amount of money in the economy decreases, the price of goods will fall resulting in deflation. If you have money saved, the falling prices mean you will be able to buy more with it so deflation is good for you. Inflation punishes savers and deflation benefits savers. That is why the bankers fear deflation, because it is good for you and bad for them. Inflation is good for them and bad for you. This is the mechanism that bankers and politicians use to steal from you. If you are deep in debt then inflation will benefit you since you are paying back the debt with cheaper money at a later date. This is basically how inflation and deflation work, nothing more complicated than that. Why does all of this matter? The government has a lot of debt and they want to pay it back with cheaper money. The easiest way to have cheaper money is to keep printing lots of it. This causes inflation which we know is bad for savers. When governments keep printing lots of money eventually people decide they don't want to hold it for very long because inflation is robbing them of buying power. As this cycle continues the money held by people gets spent faster and faster which is called the velocity of money. Eventually so much money is created driving prices to insane levels that no one wants to accept it in exchange for goods. This is how hyperinflation happens. The price of certain goods may fluxuate depending on their seasonal availability. The price increase of a few products during seasonal availability is normal based on supply and demand. When all prices start to raise at the same time this is an indication of inflation and you will notice it especially when you buy groceries every week. If the production of goods increases along with the creation of money prices will seem to remain stable. This is what people see during boom times, but when the economy slows down resulting in fewer goods being produced but money creation continues, then prices begin to rise. There are hybrid situations where some things like houses and boats will suffer from depressed prices while items like food and energy suffer from high prices. This is caused by manipulation of the markets by bankers and politicians. They try to prop up asset prices in a depressed sector like housing but the money they print flows to commodities instead causing higher prices in the things that people must have. What does this all mean? If the government continues to print lots of money it will cause high inflation if not hyperinflation. This will destroy the buying power of the money that you have saved eventually making it worthless. The U.S. government through the FED is now printing money at an increasing rate. If this continues the money you now have saved will lose all or most of its value in the next few years. The only way to preserve the purchasing power of your money during times of high inflation is to store it in tangible items that you can actually use. This may be in food, household goods, clothing, or precious metals. Many people argue that precious metals are a bad investment and that may be so normally. The thing these people don't understand is that precious metals are not an investment but a tool to preserve wealth. An ounce of silver or gold will buy about the same amount of goods that it would 200 years ago. Precious metals hold their value over time while paper currency does not. What is going to happen in the future? That is a good question that many are speculating on. This is how I see it. If the government keeps printing money it will eventually cause hyperinflation. Once hyperinflation has wiped out all of the bad debt and the savers in society the country will fall back into a deflationary depression. This is because once all of the paper wealth has been destroyed nobody will have any money left to buy anything. If this happens the people that were able to preserve even a small portion of their wealth will be rich by most people's standards and will be able to find a lot of bargains. Basically, tangible goods, fully owned real estate and precious metals will survive the destruction but anything held in paper assets will be destroyed. The government may step in at a late date and revalue the currency before it is completely destroyed but anyone holding paper assets will still take a big loss. Each person will have to decide for themselves what may happen and take the necessary precautions but if the worst happens the people cannot say they were not warned.

Another thing people need to keep in mind during high inflation is that a lot of our currency is held outside of the country. This is because the U.S. Dollar is the world reserve currency. This means that all major commodities in the world are priced in dollars. Other countries have to exchange their currencies for dollars in order to buy things around the world. Because of this foreign countries keep a lot of dollars in their banks. All we have to do to buy goods is to print more money. If the U.S. looses reserve currency status all of these banks will dump their dollars and these dollars will return to the U.S. causing the money supply to increase adding to inflation. This will also mean that we will have to convert our currency into another form to buy things around the world. The more inflation we have the more dollars we will need to convert into other currencies. This means ALL of the things we import will become much more expensive. Because we don't produce a lot of the things we use anymore our standard of living would drop considerably. This lack of money to buy foreign goods would mean shortages in the U.S. of basic necessities to include food and oil. We could no longer just print money to buy things. Like other countries now, we would have to sell more goods overseas to make money to buy imported goods. With our manufacturing base all but destroyed this would be impossible in the short term. Now that China has most of our manufacturing technology it would be difficult to compete with them. The loss of reserve currency status would mean a very difficult future for us.

4
Abandon Ship

In the near future the vast majority of people living in the cities will realize that it's no longer practical or possible to continue living there. The infrastructure that sustains them will cease to function efficiently and deteriorate due to its unsustainable nature. No longer will food and water be brought in and sewage and garbage carried out. The increasingly lower standard of living will force most to seek a more sustainable and productive living in the rural areas where resources are available and overcrowding is not a problem. More business will be conducted locally as the cost and lack of fuel makes long distance transport uneconomical and difficult. Trade skills will once again dominate as people seek to capitalize on the populations unfulfilled needs. Many lost skills will have to be relearned as people are forced to live at a subsistence level far below what they are accustomed to. As the wealth of this once great nation is slowly drained away, the masses will revolt in the face of the pain that will be visited upon them. For two hundred years the wealth of this nation steadily increased by a measure that had never been seen before. For the last few decades this has been reversed and the nation's wealth is being drained away much faster than it accumulated. As the nation's wealth is destroyed, few realize the consequences of their folly. Once the destruction is complete it will take many decades to rebuild what once was. Those who don't see the destruction happening and take actions to preserve wealth and production resources will have a difficult time in the years ahead. They will have no one to blame but themselves for the misery they will endure. If the people learn from their mistakes they will be able to rebuild their standard of living slowly but if they choose to blame others and simply wait for someone else to fix things then the poverty that results could be perpetual in its duration. This nation, with all of its natural resources, could become a permanent third world nation with no hope or future for its people. It is conditions like this that spawn dictatorships. While no one can predict the future, it will be written in the will and determination of its people. Only they can decide the fate that awaits them in the dark days ahead. Only their trust in each other and providence will lead them through to a safe haven.

5
Plan Now Don't Panic Later

When economic hard times appear, it can devastate all of the best laid plans for the future. A prudent person always has a backup plan for disruptions in the economy or in his own life due to unforeseen occurrences. But what if a catastrophic occurrence happens on a large scale during your lifetime, something that may only happen once in several generations? When this happens your backup plan may fall far short of what your family needs and you will have to deal with it. The crisis of 2008 is still playing out and already many people find themselves and their family homeless and destitute, not knowing where the next meal will come from and struggling to shelter themselves from the elements. The large number of tent cities springing up from coast to coast is a testament to people's unpreparedness to deal with catastrophic occurrences. A backup plan may be as simple as saving a few months worth of living expenses and storing some extra food to get through a crisis and this will usually be sufficient for most families until things get better. But what if things continue to get worse and stay bad for years instead of months as usual? That is the situation that people now have to deal with and none planned for. Before when one spouse lost a job the other could pay most of the bills with their paycheck until a new job was found, but today both spouses are losing their jobs and no new jobs are available. People are using up their savings and jobless benefits hoping things change before they run out of money. For some the money has already run out and those people find themselves homeless and unable to buy food and provide basic necessities for their family. The problem is that most people run things out as long as they can, and don't try to come up with a plan until they have no resources left to work with. No plan works equally well for everyone but the following steps can work for many who take the appropriate steps early enough. The main requirement for this plan is for people to recognize the end result they face while they still have some savings to use. Persons that have family or friends that can take them in have more options and may fare better than most but this plan is for those that will have to rely on themselves for basic necessities. The plan has different levels depending on how much money you have to work with. Hopefully by looking at this plan and taking a realistic look at where you stand you will be able to decide when to pull the plug on your current situation and put the plan into effect. The most difficult part is deciding that you are at the point that you must decide on a course of action and will be locked into it. Many people will not want to make this mental leap and realistically access their situation and decide they must drastically change the way they live. Some will decide to continue as normal in hopes that it will all work out, and those are the ones that most likely will be left without resources to care for their family.

6
A Mobile Castle Without A Mortgage

One thing everyone needs regardless of who they are is shelter. The best way to insure your family has shelter no matter what is to buy a good used RV or camper trailer. These can be found very cheap for now and offer you a good shelter year round for the whole family. The alternative is a tent and you really don't want to have to resort to that level of living. If you get an RV it should be an older one that you can reasonably work on yourself. Even if you can't usually someone you know probably can and an older vehicle may not cost as much to repair and maintain if it has fewer electronic parts to go bad as many of the newer vehicles do. If you get a camper trailer, which is my personal choice, you will need to go over it and make sure all systems are properly serviced and working. This will also necessitate you having a vehicle to tow it. If you currently have a vehicle and it is paid for then great but don't rely on having that vehicle if you are unable to continue making payments and lose it. In this department an older pickup truck is best. Something in the 70's or early 80's would be best maintenance wise. Also a pickup truck would give you extra storage space in the rear if you add a camper shell. You want to go over the vehicle and insure it will get you where you want to go when you need to go. Older pickup trucks are also available rather cheap, but to get a good one you will have to shop around. One of the great things about this country is that a lot of people have used pickup trucks for many years for work trucks so there is a large supply out there. If you are able to add a second or larger fuel tank it will be beneficial when the time comes that you really need the vehicle. The tank should be kept full and treated with fuel stabilizer so you won't have to rotate it as much and it will be ready to go on a moment's notice. Having a good supply of fuel will help insure you can get out of harm's way and you won't have to worry about buying any fuel immediately, which is helpful if fuel is expensive or hard to find. You should also buy some spare parts to keep in the vehicle. Things such as electrical components, hoses, belts, fluids and anything else you determine that might leave you stranded in the road. Stocking these things now will save you money on future cost increases and allow repairs when you don't have the extra money otherwise.

The next thing you will want to do is to buy a year's supply of basic foods and household goods to store in your trailer. This is an important thing you need to do and could be done before or in conjunction with the purchase of a trailer and tow vehicle. This should be enough to provide two basic meals to each family member each day for a year. If you can afford to store enough for three meals a day then that is better but this supply will insure that you won't have to go without food which is the main goal. It doesn't have to be anything fancy just stuff your family will eat and you can keep rotated until it is needed. You should stress things like flour , cornmeal , rice , dried beans , pasta , powdered milk , canned vegetables and fruit , canned meats , toilet paper , soap , laundry powder , unscented bleach , dish soap and tooth paste. You need to have basic cooking items on hand such as yeast, baking powder, corn starch, shortening and spices to cook from scratch. If you do not know how to prepare meals from scratch then you need to get a cookbook and learn now. This is the cheapest way to provide food for your family. This food supply will carry you over until you can adjust to your situation. It will give you time to think and plan in a calm manner. It can help bridge the gap between losing a job and finding another and will allow you to spend the limited resources you have on other things like shelter.

The next thing you should do is to buy two or three complete sets of durable cloths for each member of the family to include socks, shoes, underwear, shirts, pants and jackets for warm and cold weather. These should be stored in containers in the trailer and rotated out to allow for fast growing children. This will provide you with durable clothing to use in an emergency. If you are unable to purchase new clothing for a long period then this clothing could make all the difference in your standard of living. Additionally, if you should suddenly lose your home to disaster, then this supply will help bridge the gap until you can purchase more.

7
Silver Linings

Once these things are taken care of you should consider buying about $30 in face value junk silver and about 30 ounces of silver bullion coins. In a serious situation you will be able to trade for things you need when paper money may not be accepted. Even if paper currency is still good, you will be able to sell the silver as required to purchase essentials as you need them. It will provide you with an inflation hedge in bad times and act as a backup savings account. Also having several rolls of quarters to use in vending machines and a few hundred in cash would be beneficial if you have the means. If you are concerned about hyperinflation, economic collapse or currency devaluation then you can also store rolls of nickels. You can get them for face value and the current composition of copper/nickel makes them worth more for their metal content than the face value. This makes them a good store of wealth because they will never be worth less than their face value which makes them a deflation hedge and in the case of high inflation they will command a higher price than face value because of their metal content. This is the same situation we now have with pre 1965 silver coins which are worth more for their metal content than their face value. Because of this one investor recently purchased one million dollars worth of nickels as an inflation hedge. Another factor which may come into play is a currency devaluation where old money is handed in for new money at a reduced exchange rate. In times like this usually the coinage in circulation, because it comprises a smaller percentage of overall money in circulation and is very expensive to change, will retain its face value. That means that a dollar bill may lose say half of its value becoming worth fifty cents while a dollar worth of coinage will retain a dollars worth of buying power. Because of the currently devaluing dollar the U.S. mint is now proposing changing the metal content of nickels to steel which is a lot cheaper. So, if you want to store up some real nickels you had better do it soon. This is a clear indication of what is happening to our currency. Currently, silver is a better buy than gold. The ratio of gold to silver available on earth is about 1:16. This means that one ounce of gold is worth about sixteen ounces of silver. The current ratio is about 1:50. This is a distortion in the market for many reasons. The price of gold and silver gives the average person a reality check on the value of paper currencies. Because of this, it is in the governments' best interest to keep the price of precious metals down. Some have charged that the price of precious metals has been manipulated to keep it low to hide the fact that paper currency is inflating at an increasing rate. This can be accomplished by large short positions taken by major banks using ETF funds as leverage. This seems to be what is happening. The large sudden movements by precious metals are an indication of manipulation and not normal market forces. The silver market is much smaller than the gold market so it is easier to manipulate. Most of the gold ever mined on earth is still in existence. Silver is more widely used for industrial purposes and as a result most of the silver that has ever been mined has been used in the manufacture of products. Most of the silver is used in such small amounts that it is not recovered when the products are discarded. This means that there is actually less silver in existence now than gold. This fact alone means the price of silver should be much higher than it is. The distortions from manipulation in the market will eventually be overcome by free market forces. The market is much more powerful than any short term manipulation and when the market finally corrects, the real market price of gold and silver will be much higher than anyone would believe. This is based on the increasing amount of paper money that is being produced. Keep in mind, the value of gold and silver never actually change. The thing that changes is the price of the metals in fiat money. Because of these things, silver will probably correct much more than gold in the future so holding some of your wealth in the form of silver is a good way to preserve it.

8
Plan 2.0

The next level of planning would be to purchase a small piece of land in a rural area that you can park your trailer on if needed and grow some of the food you will need. An acre or two of land can still be bought for two or three thousand dollars but you will have to hunt around a bit. A few acres to live on, grow a garden and plant some fruit trees on will provide you with needed resources in the future. In a truly serious economic situation this is the best insurance you and your family can have. After purchasing the land you will want to do some position improvement such as planting a small orchard, building a 12 x 20 storage shed and building a small chicken coop. A good storage shed with a concrete floor could also serve as a small cabin to live in if you do not have a trailer and the situation required it. Also, a small flock of chickens can keep you fed when everything else fails preventing you from becoming desperate. You would also be wise to build a 4' x 8' privy/shower to use instead of your trailer toilet so you won't have to worry about disposal of the chemical affluent. A good alternative would be to install a composting toilet in the trailer. These things can assure that you can continue to take care of your family even under the worst circumstances. After these things are achieved, if your finances permit you might want to have a well drilled if you don't already have one and purchase a small lawn and garden tractor with garden implements or at least a rotor tiller to work your garden. Some of these things can be found used at a great savings. An alternative to buying a travel trailer or RV would be to buy a piece of land and put a mobile home on it. These can be found used for a few thousand dollars and offer more living space. This is a good alternative but you would not be as mobile and would be locked into one location.

9
Your Security Blanket

One thing you seriously need to consider is protection for your family. If the situation gets bad everywhere then you might have to protect your family and your property from thieves looking to take anything they can get. Many people do not like guns and that is a personal choice you will have to live with if a situation arises. Things such as mace or stun guns may be effective to a point but offer little protection if attacked by a group of determined men. If you need to get a firearm and can only afford one then your best choice would be a shotgun. You can use this for hunting and for home defense due to the various loads you can get but it is not ideal in a standoff situation with multiple armed individuals where a rifle of large caliber would be better suited. A shotgun with a good supply of ammo would give you a great deal of capability but not complete defense capabilities. Still if you had only one weapon this should be it. If you have the ability to own more weapons, a good pistol and at least one rifle would be beneficial. A good pistol for defense is the Colt .45 automatic. It is a popular pistol caliber and it has a lot of stopping power. A good thing about this gun is that you can buy carbine kits for them making them into a small rifle which has better accuracy at a distance than the short pistol barrel. This system might be a good solution for a person that is unable to handle a large caliber rifle. A good rifle caliber is the .223 or .308. The .308 is better for long range and is able to take down larger game than the .223 so it would be a better caliber to have if you only have one rifle. There are many good rifles on the market so you will need to determine which model will suit your needs. You need to make sure you have sufficient ammo, cleaning supplies and magazines for all of your weapons. Learn to be proficient with your weapons and how to maintain them properly so you will get many years of use out of them.

10
The Wrap Up

With careful shopping all of the above mentioned can be done on about $15,000. If you exclude the land and improvements you could do the first part of the plan for about $8,000. If you find some good deals you may even accomplish the first part for less than $4,000. This should be a minimum goal. It would be a good idea to keep abreast of the current price of the things listed so you can adjust the amount over time to compensate for the current market price. The plan should be when your finances get to the minimum level of enacting the plan it will be time to make the critical decision. Do you enact the plan or do you continue to hope for the best until your money runs out and you lose everything. These funds may allow you to continue your current standard of living for several more months, but then what? These are the questions you need to ask yourself now while you have the resources to protect yourself. It may be a decision at some point to not pay the mortgage and use that money to enact your plan. You need to do the math now and have a plan ready to enact when you hit a certain economic point. It will be difficult to suddenly leave the normal life you have and make this sudden drastic change but you need to think of your family's future welfare. Surviving with a moderate standard of living until you can rebuild your economic base should be your goal. This plan will provide you with a decent standard of living until you can improve things. Living in a trailer my not seem like a very good choice but would you rather have your family sleeping in a tent in the dead of winter or hope for space in a homeless shelter? That is the reality a lot of people are facing right now because of lack of planning. You do not want to be put in this position because it offers you very few choices. To tie this entire plan together it might look something like this. You find a good used trailer for $3,500 and an old pickup truck for

$1,500. You stock it with $1,000 worth of food and basic household goods and $500 worth of new clothing. You service and upgrade the truck and trailer. If you have available funds left after this you might buy some silver for an inflation hedge. After that you might want to get a shotgun and 500 rounds of ammo. If you have about $3000 in funds available at this point you would look for a piece of property in a rural area that you like. If you purchase land ahead of time, it should be in an area that you might like to vacation in during the summer which would give you a dual use for the property. If you have about $1,000 available at this point you would do the position improvements to the property as described. Finally you would install a well and get gardening equipment. You may decide to wait until the last possible minute to put this plan into action but if you do it ahead of time you will not have lost anything and you will have more time to find good deals on the things you need. If things do improve you still get to eat the food you bought and the trailer can be used for your summer vacation at the rural property you own. The silver can be sold at any time to recoup your investment and the gun can be used for hunting or skeet shooting at your property for recreation. Nothing here is really a waste unless you simply hate the country. In any event you can still sell the land, trailer and truck at any time so very little if any money is ever lost. If the worst should happen and you should lose your jobs, your savings, your vehicles and your home you will not be destitute as many are. You will have shelter, land, food, clothing and some wealth in the form of silver. One word of caution here though. If you lose everything and are forced to declare bankruptcy then you could lose all of your backup items. If you are forced to fall back on these items as a last resort then it's safe to assume you may be bankrupt. To protect these items you may want to put all of these things in a trust so that you technically don't own them. You could also put the items in your children's names so that they own them. A good lawyer could give you more insight into this type of strategy. This would insure that you would not lose them along with everything else. This plan would give your family a place to call home where you would have an opportunity to rebuild your life. You would have a place to live rent free and your food supply would give you a year to find new employment or at least start a garden and start canning some food. Even if you were 100 miles from a major city and did eventually find a new job there, you would save a considerable amount of money by having a paid for homestead to live on until you could save up the money to buy or rent a place near town. Driving 100 miles to work each day may seem crazy but I know people who do it. It would also only be for a short while until you could save the funds to move. If it is that big of a deal you could buy or build a camper body for your truck and stay in town in it during the week and drive home on the weekends. I did something similar when I had a job for several months that was a three hour drive from my home. As I said earlier, this plan gives you resources to work with to improve your situation. With a small investment you can prevent from being completely wiped out financially and give yourself a chance to recover. Another thing to consider is that you may be able to find employment in the country and eventually build a house on your land without getting a mortgage. How great would it be to be debt free and living in your own home? Even in the worst case you will have the ability to grow some food and possibly enough to sell for a modest income to take care of any bills that you do have like taxes and insurance and the things you cannot provide for yourself. Many people do not realize how cheaply they can live and still maintain a good quality of life. That is the main thing, to keep a good quality of life. With the current downturn I think many are going to have to adjust the hard way. Don't let this be you. As you can see, it doesn't take a lot of money to disaster proof your life and give you some breathing room so you can recover with the least amount of pain and adjustment. This plan should be seen as a primer to get you thinking and planning before it's too late to act. Some people might say that they have already fallen past the minimum point in the plan and have little or no resources to carry out a plan like this. If you are about to become homeless and have few resources then one course of action might be to sell what you can and get enough money to buy an acre of land in a rural area. If you have a paid for vehicle worth several thousand dollars you may need to sell it and use the money to buy land and a much cheaper vehicle so that you will still have transportation. This will at least give you a place to call your own where you can pitch a tent and do some position improvement where you won't have to deal with the kinds of people you would encounter in a tent city type of environment. You will have the ability to establish some sanitation infrastructure, plant some food to keep you fed and accumulate some materials to build a hard shelter. With as little as $600 you can build a small cabin that will keep you sheltered until you can get something more suitable. A rammed earth shelter with a tarp roof is better than a tent and you can slowly improve your shelter as time and materials permit. Living in a sod house is not glamorous by any means but our ancestors did it and made do until they could improve their situation. The biggest problem I see with people today is when they lose everything they refuse to accept the reality and expect to continue living as always and expect someone or something will come along and make things normal again before they have to suffer any deprivation. An acre of land may not seem like much but it is one of the greatest resources you can have if you only learn to use it to its maximum potential. Anyone can raise some fruit, vegetables or eggs to sell for a few dollars to get by for a while. With property you can start a small business like welding, a barber shop or small engine repair to help turn over some money. In a situation like this, a hobby or seldom used skill can pay off in a big way. Everyone should have a second vocation to fall back on in lean times. If you have no job but have a stable living condition, now would be a good time to learn a new trade while you have the time. If you are able you should take a course at a local community college to learn some trade skills. You need to keep your eyes open for opportunities to generate income and increase your wealth. Having lived in the country most of my life I can tell you it's not hard to acquire the things you need many times for free. Sometimes you can find old cars for free just for removing them from someone's yard and a lot of times they will run or maybe just need a motor or transmission which you can usually find used rather cheap. For little or no cash outlay you can have an operational vehicle which will increase your resources and capabilities. The same can be said for building materials. If you happen to be in the right place at the right time you may be able to get some used wood just for hauling it away. This is where being friendly with the locals can really pay off. They might not be able to give you a job but are usually willing to tell you how to get more from your garden , care for or butcher livestock or give you a hand fixing something , all for merely asking. The same can be said for construction sites in the city. You can find a lot of good lumber and masonry at job sites, many times just for the asking. Dumpster diving is also something that is becoming vogue these days and these people are telling of amazing finds so why not give it a try. When all else fails you need to use your imagination and be creative. If you can't find a camper trailer you may be able to find a used van body truck that is cheap enough that you can fix up inside like a camper. If you have some carpentry skills you may be able to build an enclosure that you can set on a small cargo trailer for use as a temporary shelter. Use your imagination. When you look at something don't just see it for what it is, see it for what else it could be.

11

Do More With Less

Saving money or living inexpensively does not mean you have to have a lower standard of living. You can actually have the same standard of living making $10,000 a year as someone that makes $40,000 a year just by producing more of the things you use instead of buying them. A normal middleclass person pays about $1,200 a month or $14,400 a year in rent or mortgage payments. They pay about $150 a month or $1,800 a year in electricity. They spend $120 a week or $6,240 a year in food. An average person uses about 500 gallons of gas a year at a cost of over $1,600 a year. If you could eliminate these expenses while still having all of these products you could save over $24,040 just in these four areas. By building and owning a paid for home , producing your own power , growing most of your own food and producing your own fuel you can save this much money allowing you to make only $10,000 a year and live as well as someone making $40,000 a year. The taxes you pay on 10k a year will also be much less than the taxes on 40k a year which is a hidden savings. The key to this kind of savings is taking the time to learn how to produce stuff yourself. Learn how to fix your own car, cook from scratch or repair worn clothing. A little bit of knowledge can go a long way so read and learn as much as you can whenever you can. We'll talk more about this later.

12
Greener Pastures

Up until the mid 20th century, a large portion of the population lived on farms and produced most of the things they needed internally or in the local economy. Today most people are dependent on production many miles away or even from other continents for all of life's necessities making them vulnerable to supply disruptions or internal disruptions such as unemployment or sickness. Most depend on being employed by others and making enough to pay rent or mortgage, food, utilities, transportation and repairs, healthcare, clothing and various insurance. If you fall short on any of these items or lose access to any of them for a prolonged period of time, it could mean severe deprivation or catastrophe to your standard of living. As many who have lost their jobs and not been able to find new employment can attest to, these things can happen and the suffering brought on families can be painful. It only makes sense for the head of the family to plan and prepare for bad times just as you would for hurricanes and tornados. One of the problems with modern life is that people have been taught not to worry about things such as currency collapse or depression because they have been told the government has everything under control and nothing like that could happen. Anyone who understands history knows that bad things do happen and continue to happen because we like to forget history and pretend that things are different now. As long as people are in charge of large systems we will continue to have disruptions because people are not perfect and will continue to make mistakes even when they have the best intentions. This means you need to be alert and plan ahead so you are not caught up in one of these disruptions. The well being of your family depends on you and how well your coping mechanism is designed. The U.S. population has gotten away from its roots as a manufacturing center and devolved into a service economy. People cannot create wealth by mowing each other's lawn. Wealth comes from producing a product to sell. This is what creates wealth and stability. It is true for nations and it is true for families. The best way to ensure a good standard of living for your family is by having a product to sell or at least producing a great deal of the things you need to maintain a good quality of living. Those that are dependent on an office job that may go away in bad times may have little or nothing to fall back on in a contraction. Even those that thought they had plenty put aside may find it doesn't go as far as they thought. Being without income for several years and/or having your retirement account take a big loss can leave you with few options and not much in the way of living expenses. Only about 2 percent of this nation lives on farms anymore and most of them don't produce a lot of the things they use. These factory farms are dependent on income and retailers for most of their needs just as their city cousins are. This is why I believe the most rational thing someone can do is decide to move their family to a rural area and set up a small diversified family farm. This can provide you and your family with all of the basic necessities you need and it can provide you with income from farm products above and beyond anything you may make at an external job. If you lose your job you have a backup income in farm products. You will also have a paid for home, food for your family, less transportation cost to worry about and the ability to produce some or all of your own energy. This capability will enable you and your family to hunker down and ride out the disruptions as long as they last and maintain a decent standard of living. If 15 to 20 percent of the families in this nation were to return to family farming it would eliminate a lot of the joblessness and poverty we suffer from. It would be a national security asset because there would be a lot more localized production which would help eliminate potential supply disruptions across the nation. Those that say this is crazy and would never work should keep in mind that in 1787 in the U.S., most of the population lived on a farm. These Americans ate better than most do today and unemployment was unheard of. Having this many people self employed and producing food would eliminate a lot of the competition for factory jobs. With city jobs decreasing because of a national slowdown this would take a lot of pressure off of the social structure. There would no doubt be a lot of resistance to this plan from large corporations and government because it would mean their losing some of their control on the people and this should be looked at as a positive result for the people. With as little as 6 acres a family can produce most of the necessities they need to live a healthy and prosperous life. One thing that can be said for this idea is that no matter what happens in the world people will need to eat. It's the most important occupation in the world and will continue to be. After getting your land you may decide to raise more vegetables or livestock than you need and create a cash income with the extra. If you plan to make cash income from your land you may want at least 6 acres. This will give you the space you need to be diversified and create enough extra to be worthwhile. You need to have a basic plan for your homestead before you start so you know what piece of land will work best for you. You may not find the exact land you are looking for but your plan will help you get close. You need to decide the size and layout of the house you want. What size does your garden need to be and what will you plant in it? Will you have any fruit trees and what type will be best for your area? Do you plan to have any nut trees in the yard and what type will they be? What type of livestock do you want, how much do you want and will you be able to grow enough of your own grain to feed them? Do you want some bees so you can produce honey? How about plants like grapes and currants? Will you have a berry patch? Will you be able to grow enough grain for your own needs, feed your animals, and have extra to sell and perhaps some to make your own energy? What grains do you need to grow, how much of each type and what will your rotation look like? How will you store the extra? Would a small pond be beneficial to your plan? What equipment will you need and how much will it cost? These all seem like daunting questions if you are just starting out but if you take them one at a time it won't seem like that much and you'll be surprised how quickly you can come up with a list. If your acreage is small you may only have room for some chickens, ducks, geese and rabbits. With a little more room you could support a few hogs and dairy goats. Even if you only have poultry and rabbits, this can supply all of your meat needs. A rotor tiller may be enough to provide your tilling needs or you may decide some old farm equipment would be more productive and within your budget. No two homesteads will be exactly the same. Most of the decisions you make will be based on personal preference. Starting a homestead is a big job. You can plan it out first, make a list of everything you will need and then prioritize the list based on what you can afford and will need first, and then you will be able to build it up little by little. This is not something you can do all at once unless you are independently wealthy. If you come up with a good plan you can start acquiring infrastructure before you ever buy your land. When you do finally buy your property you may have most of the equipment you need to get started. Most of the equipment you will need to get started will fit in a small shed. Planning is important so you will be able to get started with the minimal amount of equipment and cost. Some of your initial equipment purchases may look like this. For basic garden tools you might need a shovel, hoe, rake, digging fork, broad fork, post hole diggers, sickle, baskets or buckets and a supply of seeds. For chickens you might need a brooder pen , heat bulb and fixture , waterer , feeder , can to store feed in , granite grit , ground oyster shell , dusting powder , adult feeder , adult waterer, hen house , wire for enclosed run and cleaning supplies. To butcher your chickens, a chicken cone, hatchet, dipping bucket to heat water, a good set of knives and a table for dressing the birds on. To preserve your food by canning you will need a water bath canner, a pressure canner, canning jars, canning lids, extra supply of canning lids, canning utensils, canning book and canning salt. You may want certain spices and additives for certain things but you can get those things when you decide exactly what you will can. Some things will store better than others. Just these few things will provide you with meat, eggs and vegetables for the entire year. To provide you with a cheap dependable source of heat for heating and cooking you may want to invest in wood heat. A good wood stove can save you enough in one year in heating costs to pay for it depending on how much you put into the system. It also provides you with a heat source for cooking if the power goes out. You will need a stove, stove pipe, cleaning tools, ash bucket, ax, wood splitting maul, a bow saw and a chain saw if you have your own trees to cut. If you buy your firewood you will not need all of these tools but it will be much cheaper if you have your own wood supply. With a chain saw you will also need a chain sharpening file, a gas can, bar lube oil, and 2 cycle oil for the gas. To plow up a large garden you might need a rotor tiller. If the area you plant is very large you may want a garden tractor with the necessary implements to make your job faster and easier. The amount of equipment you need beyond this will be determined by how much you decide to do with your homestead. But as you can see, the amount of equipment you will need to get started and be able to sustain yourself in a basic way is not really that much.

13
The Economic Model

Many of the social ills we have to deal with today are a direct result of the abandonment of an economic model that works. In the 1960's, a suburban middleclass family had a relatively good standard of living. They had a car, or two, a nice home, quality furniture, TV's, radio's , telephones , quality clothing , a kitchen full of appliances and a job that allowed them to save some money and possibly go on a nice vacation each year. A lot of people have many of these things today but most of it is bought on credit that the person may never be able to pay off, especially at the ridiculously high interest rates that they have to pay. To have a standard of living near that of a 60's era family you have to be one of the upper middle class or even rich today. You can thank the FED for this as they are the ones that have inflated the money away. The middle class is slowly being bled into poverty and most people will not realize it until it's too late. The main differences between the 60's and today lies mainly with inflation, the technology and our production base. The technology has allowed better communication and medical diagnosis but the basic necessities are much the same. This country used to produce most of the things we used and had enough extra to export, allowing money to flow into the U.S. from abroad. This helped make the U.S. a rich nation. Today we import most of what we use and money flows out of the U.S. making us poorer and others richer. The production base allowed many to have a good working class wage and inflation was kept in check by the gold standard. That changed in 1971 with the abandonment of the gold standard. This allowed us to print money instead of making products to sell. If a person today were to live with only 1960's era products, that person would have a good standard of living by most accounts even though they didn't have the newer technology. A lot of the older products are still available today at garage sales and second hand stores at low prices because many have replaced those items with newer products even though the old ones were still serviceable. A person could buy a lot of the older products and furnish a house cheaply and get the same enjoyment and use at a much lower price. This is the best way for someone just starting out in life to build a good standard of living and stay within their budget. As your savings increase you can upgrade to newer things at a modest pace while allowing yourself to save for the future. If you can resist being caught up in the newer is better instant gratification trap, you can come ahead in life a lot faster. Another difference between then and now is that most of our production has gone overseas along with the good pay those jobs provided. This has forced many to go into lower paying lower skill jobs with less chance for advancement. When you replace jobs with fewer, lower paying jobs how can you expect anything other than a decline in the standard of living for the nation as a whole. If you are one of the working class, dependant on a good job to provide a decent standard of living for your family, you will be fighting an uphill battle for the rest of your life if you try to live the current type of conventional life. In the economic situation we find ourselves in, you need to think unconventionally.

The best way to maintain a good standard of living in a collapsing economy is to go retro and provide as many of your own services as you can. This will require you to combine the older products of the 60's suburban middle class family with a homestead type of mentality. The products don't have to be from the 60's they could just as easily be from the 80's. The point is to use the older cheaper products as a basic standard of living that you won't have to drop below, no matter what happens in the future. When you combine the cheaper house wares with the home production of food and energy, you will have a foundation to work from to ensure a good quality of life for you and your family. Additionally, a lot of the older products are of a better quality than the newer, imported stuff. Having a small but comfortable house that is paid for and an old but dependable car to drive might make you look poor compared to your neighbors but you will be far ahead of them economically. If you save to buy some newer products at a good price you will be better off than if you go into debt to buy things you really don't need. You need to analyze your needs and separate them from your wants. The needs must take priority in acquisition or you will not have the standard of living you should have.

One of the things I do to get ahead is to plan for future purchases. This works well especially if you are just starting out in life. Imagine a small comfortable house with nothing in it. Then go room by room and make a list of everything you would need for that room. List all items including furniture, rugs and paintings. In the kitchen list every type of pan, dish and utensil that you would need for all of your cooking needs. Once you have a complete list, go through it and check off all the things you already have. Then prioritize the rest of the list to determine which things you will need to buy and in what order you need to get them. If you do not have a home, by the time you get one you will have most or all of the things you need to furnish it. This will prevent you from having to furnish your home and pay for it at the same time. That can be very difficult without going into a lot of debt. The main thing you need to keep in mind is to live within your means and try to stay out of debt. While you are waiting to build your dream home you can read and learn how to do carpentry and masonry and hopefully by the time you are ready to build you will be able to do a lot of the work yourself. About half of the cost of a home is in the labor to build it. So you can save about half just by doing it yourself. Another large expense is the trim work inside. If you get a router table and learn how to use it you can save another large amount of money by making your own trim from rough lumber. It is not difficult to build a home for 25% to 35% of the cost if you do it all yourself. Many people will argue that they do not have the skills to build things but keep in mind that no one was born with the skills to build stuff. It all had to be learned by the people doing it at one time or another.

Another good way to save money is to buy goods today and warehouse them until you need them. This means you need to determine how much of certain things you will need over the next several years and buy it now. You will only be able to store things that won't go bad but it can save you a lot of money over time due to inflation and possible future shortages. You can store clothing, many types of food and spices, things like toilet paper, soap, household cleaners and building materials. Imagine if you had everything you would ever need stored in your basement. How much do you think you could save in future price increases and how much would it be worth knowing you won't have to earn the money in the future to buy those things? That could be important especially if jobs become very hard to find. These are the things that can insure you can maintain a comfortable standard of living no matter what the future holds in store. The money you hold can be inflated away or even stolen in many ways but holding goods that you can actually use and will need is a good way to store some of your hard earned wealth in a safe way.

A person or couple just starting out may not have many resources to draw on but this is not as bad as it seems. The first thing you need is a steady source of income. If you start out slow and build your way up to the standard of living that you want you will be able to do it faster and on a more stable foundation than if you try to borrow the funds to immediately arrive at the standard of living you want. This is what most people try to do and the debt load will cause you to spend twice as much of your hard earned money. If you get a normal 20 or 30 year mortgage you will pay almost twice the original purchase price of the house and maybe even more. That means you have to work twice as long to pay for it than if you just waited and saved to pay for it in full. That means if you buy a house for $150,000, you end up paying $300,000 or more for it if you buy it with debt. That extra $150,000 could buy you a lot of other nice things that you need, couldn't it? One way you can get the house you want is to start out slow and save for the things you want. Buy a lot or piece of property you like that you can pay cash for. Get water connected to the property or get a well drilled if it is in a rural area. Then instead of getting a loan and building a house, get a travel trailer you can afford to park on your lot. This will provide you with a home until you can save enough to have a home built. This slow approach has many advantages. You will not have the monthly debt payments to weigh you down and you will have more time to decide exactly what kind of home you want. If you lose your job you will not have to worry about losing your home. After a year or two you may decide you don't really like that neighborhood and it will be much easier and cheaper to move if you don't have a house and a large mortgage to worry about. Many people will have a hard time making the mental leap to live this way because people have been conditioned to believe that you have to look successful to the neighbors' right from day one. This behavior comes at a steep price and can be detrimental to your financial health. That's not what the bankers want you to think because they get rich off of this kind of behavior. This is a decision you need to think about and make for yourself. If you decide to save up to build the house you may decide to build smaller so you can get into it sooner. This can prevent you from buying or building much more house than you really need. This will also save you a lot in property tax every year. That's something you also need to think about. Everything you do needs to be geared toward getting the standard of living you want at the least cost. Once you have the property and a trailer to live in you can slowly build up the property. You can put in a good driveway to park your trailer on. Then you can build a garage to work on your car and store tools and other things in. You can plant some fruit trees and a garden for fresh foods. If you are worried about inflation making the cost of building materials higher before you are ready to build you can buy the building materials and store them on your property until you are ready to build. You could even have the house built little by little as you can afford it until it is complete. You may even be able to find a carpenter to do the work on the side as he has time and at a lower rate. You can save a great deal of money simply because you are not in a hurry. Use your imagination to figure out what will work best for you while saving the most money.

Another thing that eats a lot of your money is transportation. If you need a car then consider getting a good used one. A good $5,000 car will get you to work just as good as a $30,000 car but that extra $25,000 you save can buy you a lot of other things you may need more. Ideally you might want to have a good used car to go to work in and a good used pickup to tow your trailer with. This will give you a spare vehicle to use if your primary breaks down. Having an older vehicle will also make it easier to repair yourself if you choose. If you want to maintain your own vehicle and save money you might think about getting a classic car. An old mustang or camaro is a lot easier to repair than new cars and they will hold their value much better over time. This is also good for someone who cares what the neighbors think but wants to save money by having a used car. Many classic cars are available much cheaper than a new car but the nostalgia associated with a classic is viewed differently by most people than a normal used car. So you can have your cake and eat it too. If you want to go this route then you will also need to assemble a good set of tools. Do not waste your time getting a cheap set of tools because you will only waste money in the long run. You need to do some research to go this route so you can make a good choice of vehicle.

One of the things that can cost you a lot of money over time is electricity. There are many different ways to handle this problem. The easiest way to become energy independent is to not use electricity. This may not seem like a viable option to many people but it is. Many people today live with little or no electricity and they hardly miss it. It would be similar to living like the Amish. Instead of using electric lamps you would use candles or oil lamps for light. Your refrigerator could run on propane or kerosene and you would heat and cook with propane or wood. This would require a radical change to the normal mindset but it all depends on what you value most in life. This type of lifestyle requires the willingness and certain types of infrastructure. You would need oil lamps, a wood or propane stove and an absorption type refrigerator that runs on propane or kerosene. These are available but come with a price that may put them out of some peoples reach. The next best way is to get solar panels and a wind turbine to charge a battery bank. While using wind and solar to power the main power grid is fraught with problems that have yet to be answered, they are a good source of power for an independent homestead. The batteries can be connected to a power inverter to convert the 12 or 24 volt DC power into 120 volt AC power. This will give you the ability to use normal appliances in your home on a limited basis. Solar panels can last for decades with little maintenance and the same can be said for wind turbines. Normal lead acid batteries would have to be replaced every few years but are efficient and readily available at a reasonable cost. A good alternative to the lead acid battery is the nickel-iron battery. It was invented by Thomas Edison over 100 years ago and is a very durable battery. The batteries are almost indestructible when it comes to charging them and they can last for many decades. They only need the electrolyte changed every 10 to 20 years which gives you a great deal of independence from the national distribution system. The primary drawback of this type of battery is the cost and the fact that it is not as efficient as other types. With an off the grid system you may also need a backup generator for times of low battery power when the sun is not shining or the wind is not blowing. If you have a generator you need to have a supply of fuel on hand that can last you for several weeks or months and mix fuel stabilizer with it to keep it fresh and usable. If you have a propane generator or a tri fuel generator then you can store propane which will store indefinitely and could also be used for your refrigerator and stove. Propane is a great choice because it can be used for lighting, heating, refrigeration, cooking and power generation. The only drawback with it is the fact that you will need to store a large supply so you won't run out and it could be costly.

A great way to get entirely off the grid and not have to buy fuel for anything is to build a producer gas generator. This unit burns wood and produces flammable gasses that can be used to run a generator or even a vehicle or tractor. The only thing you need is a supply of wood. Twenty pounds of wood is about equal to one gallon of gas so one or two large trees could provide you with all of the energy you need for an entire year. For someone living in the country that has a small wood lot, this is a great option. You can produce your own electricity and auto fuel for the labor involved in cutting and burning the wood.

There are many ways to go about producing your own power. The more abilities you have the more options you will have. For someone with few skills and tools, solar panels or a wind turbine connected to a battery pack which is connected to a power inverter is the simplest way to go. A few solar panels can provide you with enough power for a refrigerator and some lighting. You will need to determine how much power you want and plan a system large enough to provide it. If you are a person who likes to tinker with things there are other options for producing power. If you can grow an extra half acre or more of corn you can build an ethanol still to produce your own ethanol to power a generator to charge a battery pack or even to power a vehicle. If you have a supply of wood chips you can build a producer gas system to power the generator or a vehicle. If you can't afford a regular generator you can build one to charge a battery pack. You can purchase a three horsepower air-cool motor and connect it to an automobile alternator via a fan belt, and use it to charge batteries. If you drive a vehicle on a regular basis you could put a few extra batteries in the rear of the vehicle and connect them to the vehicles charging system using a battery isolator to separate them from the vehicles battery, and let them charge while you drive. When you get home you can connect them to a stationary battery pack or inverter to provide power for your home. There are many ways to set up a power system, some being more complicated and labor intensive than others. You may find a combination of systems works well for you. Using wind or solar as a primary source of power and having a generating system powered by fuel you can produce is the best option to save money and be truly independent. Producing ethanol at home is legal on a small scale basis if a permit is obtained beforehand. Many different feed stocks can be used to produce ethanol, so your access to materials will determine which is best for you. The advantages of using producer gas are many. Even if you don't have a woodlot of your own, a lot of wood is available for free if you just look around. People are always getting rid of tree limbs and would be happy to give them to you just for hauling them away. If you have tree trimmers in your area they might be willing to give you truck loads of wood chips just to get rid of them. The only extra piece of equipment you might need is a small wood chipper if you need to grind up your own wood.

14

Your Next Job

For someone living in the suburbs or city, it might seem that the only backup type of job may be working in a store or some other service business for someone else. You need to think outside the box sometimes. Even in the city you can have a pickup truck, chain saw and a wood chipper. These things don't take up a lot of space but give you the ability to be self-employed and clear brush, trees and limbs from people's yards. Even on a part time basis this can generate a good cash flow. Add a lawn mower, trailer and a few weed trimmers and you have the equipment to provide lawn maintenance to businesses and homes. I know a lot of people that do this on a part time basis and make good money. You may be good at sewing and have the equipment to offer this service to people. If you are good with children you could have a small day care center. If you are good at sharpening things you might have a business sharpening saws and lawn mower blades. A person that is good with computers could start an internet business on some subject they know well. With a small workshop and tools a person could build furniture, repair small engines, do gun repair , do welding , repair cars , do auto detailing , bake cakes and cookies to sell , or just offer handy man services. The list is endless, but you need to determine what you like doing or what skills you have that you can generate income from. This can be your backup vocation if the worst should happen. Identify what you will be doing and get the skills and equipment you will need while you have the opportunity. You don't want to wait until you are jobless and unable to buy the things you need to start your backup job. Look around your home at the things you have. Do you have any equipment now that can be used as an alternate cash generator? The smallest things can sometimes generate a lot of cash. Think up a list of small items that won't cost you a lot but can be used to provide a service that others will need then start buying these things as you are able. Get the things you decide will help you start a part time business. I purchased a small mig welder and accessories for less than $150. Two or three small welding jobs will pay for this and I have the ability to earn a small regular income from it if necessary. Until then it can sit in the shed until I need it. A limited amount of tools can set you up to offer road side assistance. Tire changing tools, a lock out kit, some jumper cables or a jumper pack and a gas can and you have all you need to provide yourself with a full time job. You can provide this service for one or more of the national auto clubs. So you see, even in the city you have many job opportunities available to you. In the country you have the room to grow things that you can sell. Fruits, vegetables and flowers are the easiest things to start with but you may want to expand into things like honey, livestock or firewood. A small produce stand can generate a good cash flow for most of the year. You can sell flowers, fruits and vegetables in the spring and summer, pumpkins and Christmas trees in the fall and firewood in the winter. Eggs, meat, cheese, preserves, and baked goods can be sold year round. The question you need to answer is, what will people need no matter how good or bad the economy is? A few small pieces of equipment and a plan will be worth a great deal to you if it ever becomes necessary to use it. The purchase of capital equipment and the training to use it can generate a great deal of money to you over the course of your lifetime.

15
Personal Responsibility

One of the biggest problems with the society we live in is that everyone has been conditioned to believe they don't have to take any responsibility for their family, themselves or anyone else. If something catastrophic happens they think someone will show up to take care of the problem and provide them with everything they need and will make things normal again. Today most people don't know how to take care of themselves when confronted with a bad situation. How many times have you heard someone suffering from a disaster say, "Where is the government when you need them?". As the head of a household it is your responsibility to care for your family and yourself no matter what circumstances you are in. Many will try to pass the buck and blame someone else for their lack of preparedness.

Taking responsibility and being prepared for any circumstance will insure your family will not suffer unnecessary hardship that will take a toll mentally and physically. Knowing you can care for your family no matter what will give you confidence to overcome any situation no matter how desperate. Being prepared with a plan and resources will allow you to remain positive and help generate a good outcome. When your family knows that you know what to do and are not worried it will help them cope much better. As the head of the family you need to have all of the answers before times become critical. Being unprepared means you are at the mercy of nature and other people that may not have your best interest in mind. When you consider the different problems you could be faced with during your lifetime and come up with a solution to them it's much easier to be calm when everything is falling apart around you. Most people are not prepared to deal with out of the ordinary circumstances and as such their coping mechanism is fragile at best. Some people break down from nothing more than having a bad day at work. This fragile nature of our society makes it difficult and often dangerous when the norm is breached. One of the things that can breach this normalcy is the loss of a job. The interruption of income can cause havoc in a household that has not prepared for this eventuality. In normal times most people can muddle through until a new job is secured but what happens if you are living in historical times and are witness to events that are usually relegated to history books. How do you deal with events that only happen every few generations? What if job loss is compounded by some natural or manmade disaster national or international in scope? The only way to cope with out of the ordinary events is to be independent of the social network and self sufficient in areas that are critical to your survival. If you have a paid for home, can provide your own food, power, water and security then you could cope fairly well if you lost your job or were victim to a wide scale disaster. These are the basic necessities that people need to live day to day. When you cannot provide these things for yourself you are a potential victim and can face an uncertain future. You run the risk of being at the mercy of those that can provide these things for you and of being manipulated by them. To provide these things for your family is to be independent and responsible. When large numbers of people are deprived of the basic necessities they can become dangerous and will seek out those that can provide those things that they want. These people, depending on their state of deprivation, will steal and even kill if necessary to get what they need. Being responsible also means planning for this eventuality and determining how it will affect you in your area. Know when and how it could happen and have a plan to deal with it so you can keep your family out of harm's way. If you have a plan to deal with many types of disasters, you will be able to maintain your standard of living and quality of life no matter what.

16
The Family Safe

To protect your family from danger, it is good to have a secure shelter where you can go in a moment's notice. A safe room in the basement with a hidden door can protect you from tornados, hurricanes and even looters. It should be built with cinder blocks and concrete to offer good protection from flying debris or a collapsing structure. This room should be stocked with your emergency supplies and be capable of housing your family for several days or weeks if necessary. It should have at least a rudimentary ventilation system, a cooking and heating source and some type of sanitation equipment. With these items, even if your home were destroyed by wind or fire, you would be able to provide the basic necessities for your family. To provide power you could have a small generator powered by a hand crank or bicycle that charges a battery or two which are connected to a power inverter to provide AC power. This would be enough to power a few LED or compact fluorescent light bulbs, a small hot plate and even a small microwave oven. You could also have a radio and a computer that plays DVD's and games. This setup would also give you the ability to charge batteries for flashlights and other small equipment. If you have the financial means, a solar panel would tie in nicely with this setup. A safe room would provide you with a safe place to go without having to leave your home. If you don't have a basement you could build a small patio behind your home with a safe room hidden under it. Your entrance could be located under a built up planter box on one end and the ventilation system could be routed out the side of a brick BBQ. If the security situation were to break down locally then you would want to remain as invisible as possible to stay out of harm's way. These types of preparations may seem foolhardy by many who claim it's a waste of time to prepare for the end of the world. It is foolish to prepare for the end of the world because in that case there won't be anything left to survive. What you are preparing for is something less than total destruction of the planet where most people are still alive but the infrastructure that maintains us is destroyed to some degree. It happens somewhere on the planet almost every week , where an area is stripped of infrastructure in a disaster and the people cannot take care of themselves and require outside help for even the most basic necessities. If a disaster is national or international in scale, such as a currency collapse or massive solar flare which takes down the power grid, there may not be any help coming so having your own resources to fall back on would be critical to survival. A well stocked safe room that can allow you to take care of your family and emerge with enough supplies to start rebuilding your life is something that will allow you to sleep well at night. You will be amazed at the capabilities you can store in a small 10 x 16 room that can house a family of four.

There are many types of supplies that you can store to provide for your family or to sell or trade. This also applies to equipment you can use to produce goods to generate an income. What type of supplies would you want if the distribution system were shut down for a prolonged period of time? The most important supplies would be the things that you cannot produce locally that everyone needs. Things like salt, sugar, unscented bleach, toilet paper, coffee, chocolate, alcohol, medical supplies, seeds and fuels would be in great demand if the supply system went down for any reason.

Food would be the most sought after commodity and in most places, even the city, food can be grown to some degree so seeds would be a necessity. It's the things you can't grow locally that you might want to have extra of because these will command a premium. You would also want to have equipment to produce things that are not locally made like soap, candles, honey, flour, alcohol, cider/vinegar, and maybe even cloth. A welder would be good for making some types of hand tools. A bullet reloading set with dies and supplies for reloading popular calibers might be valuable in some instances. If you have a power supply you would be able to run a small 7 cu.ft. Deep Freezer. This would run for about 24 hrs with a power inverter on the power stored in a 12 volt deep cycle battery. This would be useful for keeping frozen foods and making ice which you could sell or trade. A battery charger that will recharge alkaline batteries would give you a service to offer those with battery powered devices and a limited supply of batteries. You may even be able to offer the service of recharging 12 volt batteries for people if you have the generating capacity.

The only problem with a safe room is the fact that if you lose your home to foreclosure then you lose your safe room as well. The only way to circumvent this is to have a safe room located on a piece of property that you own and won't lose if you go bankrupt. This ties in nicely with the idea of buying a small piece of country real estate. Even if you don't build a home on it, just having a garden spot, some fruit trees, a privy, a water supply and a hidden safe room will give you the infrastructure you need to care for your family.

17
The Barter Economy

Most people do not realize how the currency system is stacked against them. Our current system, which is backed by nothing tangible, is designed to enrich the few at the top at the expense of everyone at the bottom. People do not understand how this con works so they do not protest it. They only see the results and complain to the very people who run the con and are told things will be fixed soon, only soon never comes and things just continue to get worse. The people don't understand that the people who print the money, loan it to their friends. These people get to spend the fresh new money before it makes its way into the broader economy and creates inflation(higher prices).The more money that is present in the economy , the higher the price of goods have to go to balance the amount of goods available against the amount of money available. As the money flows through the economy, the increased money supply creates inflation, and by the time money gets to those at the bottom of the economy, inflation has preceded it and it holds no benefit for these people. Only those at the top that get to use the money before it creates inflation will benefit from it. This is a hidden tax on people and is the best reason for staying out of the currency system. It not only robs buying power from those who haven't earned the money yet, but also from those who have saved for the future. It destroys the buying power of the money they have already earned and ensures a lower standard of living in the future because of it. The best thing people can do is create their own local payment system until the currency system is once again backed by something tangible. During a catastrophic event, currency collapse or some natural or manmade event that makes fiat currency worthless, the creation of a barter economy is a foregone conclusion. The act of carrying around a bushel of corn for trade would be difficult enough but for a farmer with

5,000 bushels and limited transportation due to fuel shortages or non-functional equipment, it would be almost impossible. Another problem with barter is that you may not have something readily exchangeable. You may want to trade your potatoes for eggs, but the egg guy won't take potatoes, but he will take corn to make chicken feed. This may force you to make a few trades to get your eggs. This is where a medium of exchange is needed to expedite a trade. Gold and silver fill this role very well but as most people do not understand the need to hold gold and silver coins, there may not be enough coins to circulate in a given area to supply the demand. To alleviate this problem a barter exchange can be established that issues Barter Certificates (BC) to act as a medium of exchange in a community. Barter script is not a new idea and is currently used in many communities around the U.S. but most of this local script is put into circulation by buying it with U.S. dollars which would not work with a failed fiat currency. These current barter scripts are also not backed by anything physical except maybe U.S. dollars, another unbacked piece of paper. The solution to many of the problems with a barter script is to actually back it with something physical. A barter exchange can be established in a building that can be secured and has the necessary infrastructure. When you establish the exchange the more infrastructure you have the better. You may need such things as coolers and freezers for produce and meats and storage bins for things like grains and firewood. Absorption refrigeration units that run on propane are the best to have because they will continue to function after an event that knocks out the power grid or even shorts out conventional compressor units. Propane to power these units may be stored in bulk for very long periods and in the event the propane supply is cut off these units could be adjusted to run on bio gas from livestock manure. In many third world countries, they produce bio-gas to fuel their stoves for cooking, so this is a viable option. Scales of various sizes will be needed to weigh different products. Building infrastructure may be an ongoing process. Other things you may want are grain mills to produce flour and cornmeal, a butter churn, cream separator, cheese press and cheese making supplies, fruit press and any other food processing supplies that might be too expensive for the individual to buy. Farmers and individuals with food or other useful commodities can bring them to the exchange and trade them for barter certificates (BC). These certificates can be used inside or outside of the exchange to trade for work or to trade for goods and services. The face value of all certificates would be fully backed by items held at the exchange. The exchange may not have exactly what you want but at any time your certificates could be exchanged for physical items. The exchange can be set up by a small group or a single person. There should be a small board made up of local farmers and businessmen to set the value of items accepted by the exchange to insure items have a fair market value relative to other items. The exchange can produce value added products such as cornmeal from corn it took in. The cornmeal will have a higher value than the corn so certificates for the additional value can be created and held in the exchanges "account" to compensate workers or acquire needed infrastructure. If an item at the exchange spoils or is damaged making it un-exchangeable , then the value of that product will be deducted from the exchanges account in order to keep all issued certificates fully backed and redeemable. All items would exit the exchange at the same value as it entered with the exception of value added products produced by the exchange. This system would work best in a rural area but can also work in a suburban area where land is available to grow food. The exchange manager would have the job of ensuring the exchange takes in a balance of items and would need to limit what items come in and how much of each. You don't want to be sitting on 10,000 BC of lead and 10 BC of food products. With proper management the exchange could handle almost anything from base metals, baked goods and furniture to fuel, produce and meat. The capability of the exchange is limited only by the community that supports it. The exchange does not have to be limited to new items or fresh produce. Good used clothing, recycled lumber or homemade goods can be traded if the demand is there. Under good management with support from the community, the exchange could literally become one stop shopping. One might argue that this type of exchange is fine for small towns or rural areas but would not work in urban areas where little food or basic necessities are produced. They would be right to some extent. Barter is the exchange of actual goods and useful services. An urbanite that has a non-productive job shuffling papers all day (a.k.a. government employees) will not have a product or service that anyone needs in the real world, so unless they learn a skill or start producing a product people really need, they won't be able to engage in the barter economy. If you are forced to rely on a barter economy and you have no skills or products to trade, you probably won't be around very long unless you learn very quickly. That's the great thing about a barter economy; everyone is productive in some way. Even if you don't have a garden or a lot of skills to trade, almost everyone has items around their home that may have some trading value. It may be a decision whether to keep the 10 gallons of gas in the car or trade half of it for food. You don't want to be put in this position but if you have useful items you can trade until you start producing something it may buy you some time. Just having a small garden that produces some extra food and new seeds will be a huge benefit. The sad truth is that in this situation many without skills will not want to make the effort to learn and be productive, but will expect others to provide for them so prepare to turn them away if necessary. That is not to say you should not help your neighbors if you are able, especially if they have skills and were just caught unprepared at the onset of the emergency or they are physically unable to do much. The certificates should be printed and stocked so they are available in advance of an event which requires their use. They should be embossed or printed in a way as to make counterfeiting difficult. If the certificates are not printed before an event happens, the supplies and the means to print them mechanically should be on hand. I say mechanically because if the grid goes down or electronics are disabled, your computer and printer may be useless. Even better than paper certificates would be to have bronze or brass coins made in the proper denominations. These would be much more durable than paper but would have a much higher production cost. The certificates can be printed by the exchange and held in a safe. As items are brought in they are exchanged for certificates which the individual can exchange for other goods at any time. The value of the outstanding certificates will equal the value of items in the exchange at all times. If the exchange has no inventory then there should be no outstanding certificates.

The certificates can be printed in the following denominations:
1 BC
5 BC
20 BC
100 BC
.1 BC fractional
.5 BC fractional

The following is a list of how items might be valued:

1 oz. Gold = 250 BC
1 oz. Silver = 15 BC
1 Hour work = 3 BC
1 Month rent = 180 BC
30 KWH electricity = 1 BC
1 Gal. fuel = 1 BC
1 Bu. Wheat = 3 BC
1 Bu. Corn = 1.7 BC

1 Gal. Milk = 1 BC
1 Doz. eggs = .5 BC
1 lb. Cornmeal = .25 BC
1 lb. Poultry = .33 BC
1 Chord Firewood = 25 BC
1 lb. Lead = .5 BC
1 lb. Copper = 1 BC

It is also important to keep this type of exchange in private hands and not in the hands of a government entity for obvious reasons. Government entities will attempt to garner favors and gain support by keeping the unproductive masses supplied and use it as a way to control the population. If a government entity has power over an exchange at some point they will be tempted to issue unbacked certificates to their supporters. The productive individuals would soon find an empty exchange and have no ability to use their certificates and to draw certificates out of the hands of producers the government would start to tax them to help offset the unbacked certificates they produced. Does this sound familiar? That's why barter exchanges must be kept out of the hands of the government.

Since this is a local institution, if the exchange manager issues unbacked certificates, the local populace will soon find out and be able to go directly to the source for restitution. The exchange should be community or town based because transportation may be an issue and transporting goods over a long distance could be difficult or even dangerous. If nearby communities set up exchanges and coordinate their exchange values, exchanges could swap products to expand the product base and even accept each other's certificates within limits. The potential for trade between exchanges is huge and could allow large regions to reestablish trade again fairly rapidly. A town with a steel mill could exchange processed steel and steel products to another exchange for food and scrap metal. A town with a textile mill could exchange finished clothing for wool or cotton and food products. A coal mine exchange can provide coal to a power plant exchange via a railroad exchange. The foundation for an exchange system depends on agricultural products to provide the food that everyone will need. Food will be the primary commodity to keep manufacturing, transportation, mining and energy sectors on line. Without food the other commodities will have little value. If you substitute gold and silver for paper certificates, you basically have a large barter economy, which is what we used to have. If the vast majority of people ever figure this out it won't bode well for the government bureaucracy. Using gold and silver for trade puts the ultimate power in the hands of the people. By using fiat paper the government has all of the control over the people and economy. History has shown that governments always abuse this power and in the end the system collapses, many times with dire results for the unprepared people.

18

What's The Plan?

To insure their needs will always be met, people need to have a backup plan to ride out disruptions in the economy as well as for natural and manmade disasters. It does not matter where you live. Disruptions can affect you wherever you are. If you have a backup plan you may be able to stay where you are for the duration, but a severe crisis may force you to seek a more secure location to live until things improve. You need to consider the possibility that you will have to relocate and decide where that will be. That is something you need to think through now while you have the time to think clearly and research your decision. You need to think about the possible routes to get there, what type of resources you will have upon arrival and how much fuel you will need to keep on hand to get you there if you are unable to get fuel along the way.

You need to determine how much stuff you can carry and exactly what that stuff will be. Make a list and do a test load out if you can. This will give you the ability to load up quickly and evacuate with all of your essentials if you are suddenly in imminent danger. You may even want to identify more than one relocation site depending on the type of disaster you are escaping. Ideally you will be heading to a relative or friends home or even a second home that you have. If you don't have an alternate home to head to you may have selected a hotel or motel out of the danger zone and if this is the plan you may want to call before you leave and make a reservation so you don't get there to find no vacancies. If the situation is so dire that you decide to stay away from populated areas, an alternate might be a deserted site in a national forest that you have surveyed ahead of time that has a good camp site and fresh water supply nearby. This would necessitate you having the necessary camping gear and supplies to last the duration that you are there. This takes good prior planning to go this route but is not difficult if done in advance. This type of situation is where an RV or camper trailer would be very helpful. It would allow you to have most of your supplies already packed and ready to go. You would only need a short list of things you need to pack and head out the door. It would also be helpful once you got to your destination if you had a place to stay so you don't have to impose on your hosts. You would be able to set up in their driveway or yard and not have a crowded house. This would become more important as the duration of the stay increased. A small cargo trailer preloaded with supplies that is ready to hook up and go would also be a good option. If the trailer is enclosed then you might be able to use it to live in also. Even if it is not big enough to live in you could set up a small kitchen with a propane stove and refrigerator inside to make meal preparation easier. If you are handy with tools then you might want to build a small house that you can set on your trailer and fasten down. This would give you an open trailer to use under normal conditions and an enclosed structure you can load up and carry with you. If the trailer is big enough, the structure could be large enough to serve as a camper type trailer. This would be a great hobby project to work on. Another project along these lines would be to buy an old pickup truck and build a camper body on it. This would serve the same use as a camper trailer or RV just on a smaller scale.

19
Gods and Groceries

To prepare for difficult times requires a lot of the same preparations as preparing for natural disasters. When I decide to prepare for something I like to assume the worst case scenario. If you plan for the worst case imaginable, and something far less happens, then you will be able to handle it very easily. On the other hand if you only prepare for the most likely scenario with minimal resources and something far worse happens, you will be left in need of more resources than you have access to and this will cause deprivation and possibly physical harm on your part. A lot of people die every year for need of normally readily available materials like clean water , medical supplies , communication ability to summon help or warm clothing all because they failed to prepare for the emergency they find themselves in. Those that take responsibility for themselves and their family and prepare for emergencies are often times ridiculed as fear mongers and fools, usually by the same people who fail to prepare and then are forced to beg for aid when a disaster happens. Many times even after this these unprepared people will go back into the unprepared trance they live in and continue to ridicule others. The intelligent ones will usually make some preparations after this happens. Disaster preparations will be whatever you decide is prudent for your family. It should consist of certain things such as a plan , food , water , light , heat , communications , shelter(permanent and portable) , security , power , warm clothing , medical supplies ,currency and transportation. Disasters can take many forms. It can be a fire or flood that forces evacuation, a hurricane or blizzard that forces you to hunker down for a week or more if power goes out, an earthquake that disrupts services or a nuclear incident. These are the things we all call disaster but what about the mini disasters that happen to people every day that disrupt their lives. Things like fuel shortages, food shortages and power outages can and do happen all the time and can cause your family severe suffering if it continues for very long. What about the people that live paycheck to paycheck. What would one of these people do if they lost their job? How would they pay rent, buy food, pay utilities and purchase clothing? The social safety net will provide some of these things for a while and at a minimum level but what happens when they run out? If you say that society will take care of these people then why are so many homeless and living in tent cities now? How can society take care of everyone if most of society needs help? And these things are just the everyday things that are happening now. What happens if we have an unusual disaster that affects the whole country or even the world? Disasters that can change life as we know it can include currency collapse and hyperinflation, asteroid impacts, volcanic eruptions, pole shifts, massive solar flares and world war. All of these things have happened at some time on this planet and will probably happen again in the future. Some of these things may not happen for thousands of years but others can happen at any time without warning. How do you plan to deal with something like this if it happens? How do you plan to take care of your family if all available resources are cut off for weeks or months? Where will you go and what will you do if the currency collapses or you lose your job and cannot buy anything? Even if you do nothing more than sit down and come up with a plan to deal with these potential problems then you will be ahead of the general population and will be more prepared to take care of your family if something happens. Just having a plan will allow you to take immediate action to acquire the things you will need and you will be able to think in a calm manner.

And what if a mega disaster happens? You may say it would be better not to prepare and just let yourself die when it happens because life would not be worth living afterwards. The only problem is, even if one of these mega disasters happens, you probably won't be killed instantly. As a matter of fact a large percentage of the population would probably survive initially until the few surviving resources were used up. Some would say it's not right to store up supplies that others won't have. They would say it's immoral to have more than your fair share in that type of circumstance. I would say it's very moral to store extra in times of plenty when everyone has the same opportunity to acquire supplies. It's only immoral when you try to get more than your share when supplies are limited. Storing supplies during seven years of plenty to eat during seven years of famine is a strategy as old as the written word itself. So do you plan on just slowly dying of starvation or exposure to the elements? That's a slow and miserable way to die in my opinion. And do you plan to just watch your kids slowly suffer and die? Many will say they will just trust in God and he will take care of them and to prepare is to deny Gods power. If you truly believe this then I won't try to change your mind but my belief is that God gave me a brain for a reason and I don't intend to bother him by asking for help until I've done everything I can do. I would argue that God has given us everything we need to take care of ourselves on this planet so it is up to us to use it wisely. This would include the knowledge to protect ourselves from harm. If God intended to provide for us and to protect us from harm by his own doing then why did he give us the knowledge to harvest and store food , cure disease , build shelter and protect ourselves from disasters? Why does he allow people to starve, to die of curable diseases and to die in natural disasters that he can prevent? To say that you do not have to take responsibility for yourself is to deny these facts. This is not to deny Gods power but to acknowledge the power he gave us to care for ourselves and others. If you believe that a disaster or economic disruption will occur in the future then you have a responsibility to your family to be prepared so you can weather the storm. If you do not think you need to prepare for anything then you may receive help from God should something happen, but that help may be in the form of a very hard lesson that you will learn.

20
Give Me Liberty or…

Living the American dream is an idea sought by many but understood by too few. Until the masses seek to regain the freedoms now lost, the American dream will continue to deteriorate until nothing remains of it except a small footnote in history asking how we could allow this experiment in freedom to fail. As freedom is lost and is replaced by big government, the standard of living will plunge and the people will suffer the agony of third world poverty the likes of which they could never imagine. The nation has not crossed the Rubicon yet but it is in sight. If this march to oblivion is halted in time, the nation that we once knew might be revived without bloodshed. Otherwise, once that line has been crossed, nothing short of revolution and bloodshed will bring it back. This nation must have a rebirth to correct the problems we have, but the question is will it be peaceful or violent. Regardless of how the future turns out, there will be many years of strife and misery to deal with during this transitory period. To come through it families will need to go back to basics. They will need to become more self reliant and productive to fulfill their needs. This is the only way to rebuild the wealth of the nation. People will have to think creatively to overcome the challenges of the future and relearn much forgotten knowledge. The people must once again take responsibility for themselves. If the people learn from their mistakes, the nation can be prosperous once again but if not, it will be the end of the greatest experiment in history.

21
The Worst Case Scenario

As I said before, I like to plan for a worst case scenario so I don't get caught short regardless of what happens. So, what does a worst case scenario look like? Imagine this if you will.
The dollar is inflated to the point that no one wants to accept it for payment. Those that had retirement plans, stocks, bonds, cash and ETF funds now discover that those assets are worth about the cost of one loaf of bread. This is assuming that they can be cashed in and the companies did not go bankrupt like MF Global, destroying investor's assets. The people who are lucky enough to still have jobs at this point now cannot get paid and the companies cannot transact any business so the employees get laid off and the businesses close. Any cash that you still have will not buy anything so you cannot buy food, fuel, clothing and pay your rent or mortgage or your utilities. Businesses selling the items previously listed

cannot transact business due to a lack of a medium of exchange so they close. Police, firemen, doctors, power plant workers, and all of the people we depend on for everyday services no longer can get paid. Some of these people may stay on the job but most will probably stay home to care for their family. Unless power, water, hospitals and communication systems are taken over by the government and workers are forced to work you will lose power, water, medical services and communications. Most of our power plants are fueled by coal, which must be dug out of the ground and transported to the power plants by rail. Food is raised by farmers and sold to processors who then package it and send it to stores. With no medium of exchange these actions would stop. After a week or so most people will start to run out of water and food and will seek out those things that their family needs. The longer this goes on the more desperate they will get and the number of violent acts will soar. Rioting and looting will be wide spread and property destruction will be immense. For lack of clean water and proper sanitation, many will get sick. The sick and injured will have access to little or no medical help. Disease will develop and run rampant among the population. Those with medical conditions may die once their medications run out and those that take drugs for mental conditions will add to the violence and pandemonium. The dead will go unburied and add to the unsanitary conditions. Gangs will form and begin looting for supplies and raping and killing at will. With no power, fuel or communications the distribution system will cease to function. That means no fuel, food, or other necessities will get to the people who need it. Given the Government actions during hurricane Katrina, do you think they will be able to handle these problems on a national scale? All of this assumes a currency collapse. These things could also happen as a result of a massive solar flare or nuclear EMP which could take down the national power grid and render some or most electronics inoperable. On a national scale the worst violence would likely take place in the urban and suburban areas due to the fact that these areas have little or no infrastructure on a local level to produce food and water.

So how do you prepare for something like this and how do you protect your family? A plan to deal with the worst case will depend on many factors. That is to say it will depend on your location. No plan will work equally well for everyone so your plan has to be tailored to you and your situation. There are some common things that all plans will have in common. You will need a supply of clean water, food, shelter, sanitation, security, energy, communication and transportation. You can only survive about three days without fresh water so this needs to be high on your priority list. You can store bottled water, jugs or barrels of water that you fill or have a good water filter and a source of fresh water that you can access. If you have a well with a hand pump or just a shallow well that you can draw water from with a bucket, you will be in good shape.

You will need food to get you by until the distribution system is restored or you can grow your own. You can store dehydrated or freeze dried foods if you can afford it. If you are financially challenged you can slowly accumulate canned goods from the store until you have enough and then keep them rotated until you need them. Many of the foods you buy in the grocery store are dehydrated or freeze dried so you may be able to combine these with the canned goods you buy. If you have the ability to grow some food you will be able to store and can your own food indefinitely. On food storage there are three questions you need to keep in mind. How much water will I need to prepare it, will I need to heat it and how will I heat it?

Shelter is the next issue you need to explore. If you have a home, is it yours? Will you lose it if you cannot pay your rent or mortgage? Will you try to shelter in place no matter how bad things get? Do you have supplies to reinforce your home against looters? What will you do if you are forced to evacuate and what will you take with you? Do you know someone in another town you can stay with? Do you have another property you can go to? As a last resort do you have an RV or a tent you can live in? If you answer all of these questions you will have a basic plan for shelter figured out.

Sanitation is necessary if you stay in one place for a period of time. It is important because lack of proper sanitation facilities can cause illness or even death in extreme cases. Poor sanitation creates a breeding ground for disease and in a survival situation you need to stay as healthy as possible. If you shelter in place you need to know if you have your own septic system or if you are connected to a city sewer system. This is important because if you have your own system you can continue flushing your toilet as long as you can find water to put in the tank. If you are connected to a city system it will likely depend on power to pump the sewage through the line and lack of power will cause the lines to back up into your home if you continue to use it. A temporary solution may be to put a plastic liner into your toilet and dispose of it when full or to use a portable toilet that you can empty. This waste will need to be buried away from any fresh water sources to prevent contamination. If you have a small yard and some building materials you could build a privy (outhouse) in your yard. This is a simple and effective long term solution. The local zoning inspector may not permit this type of thing but in an extreme circumstance they will be the least of your worries. If you are on the move and only staying in place a few days you can dig a cat hole to utilize. This should be away from any water sources to prevent contamination and should be about twelve inches in diameter and about eighteen inches deep. This should be covered completely before you move on.

Security is necessary when society breaks down and you are forced to provide your own protection. The most effective protection you can have is a gun. This may not be possible for some because of personal beliefs or local laws so you may have to make do with mace or stun guns. If you are in a situation where you feel you need a gun for protection and you don't have one then that is a good indication you need to relocate fast. If you have a gun you need to practice with it so that you are proficient. You also need to keep a good supply of ammo on hand. How much is enough? That depends on how much shooting you do but I would suggest no less than 500 rounds be kept on hand at all times.

Energy is important in modern life. Everything we do depends on energy of some sort. This can be divided into three types, energy for heating and cooking, for electrical power and for transportation. Some fuels can be used for all of these things and they are the best to have. Propane is one of the best all around fuels because it can be used for basically everything and it will store indefinitely without degrading. The only problem with it is you cannot produce it yourself. A homemade substitute for propane would be bio-gas made from livestock manure. If you have a good wood supply, wood can provide you with all of your energy needs to include transportation, power generation and heat when you combine it with a producer gas system. For a long term situation solar and wind work well if you have the infrastructure to store and convert the power.

In times of emergency, communication is important so you know what is going on locally and nationally. It will alert you to the need to relocate and which routes are the safest. It can provide you with information from other individuals so you can coordinate your efforts. A ham radio will let you reach out around the world. A CB or small two way radio will let you stay in touch with others in your area and a weather radio will keep you alerted to local hazards. In a disaster the more information you have the better your decision making capability will be.

Transportation in a crisis could be the difference between life and death. When it's time to go you need to be able to go and not have to worry about what route to take or if your fuel supply is enough. That is why it's critical to keep a full tank of gas at all times. At the very least you should keep a few cans of gas handy in case you need it. If you cannot use your car the next best thing would be a motorcycle. This will allow you to navigate around stalled cars and traffic congestion and they get really good fuel mileage. The next level down from that would be a bicycle. These can go most anywhere and don't require any fuel. If you have a bike you might want to have a few basic tools for minor repairs and a hand pump and tire repair kit for flats. If you had to rely on one to get out of town it would help if it had baskets and maybe a small trailer you could tow. The last level of transportation would be your leather personnel carriers (a.k.a. boots). You can go many places on foot unobserved and get through dangerous areas quietly as opposed to vehicles. The main disadvantage is your speed which is greatly reduced. Each type of transportation has strong points and weak points so you need to decide which is right for you and what to use as a backup. One other type of transportation you could employ would be a boat. If you live near a body of water you may be able to use a boat to get out of the danger area if a vehicle is not available. A large boat with living quarters might be a good choice if your options are limited. This would be equivalent to using an RV as temporary shelter.

In a national breakdown, you must decide to shelter in place or move to more hospitable surroundings. If you shelter in place you need to keep a low profile and be prepared to defend your home. If you have the cooperation of others in your neighborhood you will be safer. If you live in an urban or suburban area it will be more dangerous as time goes on. The best plan would be to move to a rural area early during the crisis to insure safe travel. This would allow you to provide more of the things you need internally. An area with lower population and more natural resources would be safer and less stressful. In this situation a small group working together could get by much better than in the city. If you think this might be necessary in the future you may want to survey potential locations and meet the locals now while things are normal. Once a serious event starts many people may decide to move to a small town and you will be more welcome if the locals know you. You should locate a place to stay ahead of time. If a mass exodus happens in the cities the rural towns may be inundated by refugees and at some point they may stop letting people in due to lack of resources. In a serious event you do not want to end up a refugee. Your plan should be capable of getting you through a serious event while maintaining your safety and standard of living.

22
Closing Thoughts

The freedom that we have enjoyed for two hundred years is slipping away. Most people are so preoccupied with their daily lives that they don't notice. Those that do see what is happening try to ignore the facts and continue to hope things will get better and return to normal. For better or worse, the way we live will be very different ten years from now. Many will lose the standard of living they now enjoy unless they take proactive steps now to preserve their wealth. The system that allowed us to be so prosperous is now under attack. Free market capitalism is about the unfettered production and distribution of goods and services to meet public demand. This system is being ruled and regulated into the hands of a wealthy few whose intention is to control everything we do. This manipulation of the economy is destroying the middle class and the wealth created by them. The massive printing of money by the government is destroying the value of the dollar and it is only a matter of time before it is not accepted for goods around the world including much needed oil. If this is allowed to continue the vast majority of Americans will live the rest of their lives in poverty and despair. The only way to insure a good quality of life for your family in the future is to become more self sufficient and leave the consumer based life behind and become a producer. Your future is up to you. Good luck.

Resource and planning Guide

Food Storage Items

Flour
Cornmeal
Oatmeal
Pancake mix
Vegetable oil
Salt
Baking powder
Corn starch
Baking soda
Sugar
Dried beans
Powdered milk
Potatoes
Syrup
Honey
Molasses
Rice
Canned ham
Mac & cheese
Spaghetti
Corned beef
Gravy mix
Canned vegetables
Canned fruits
Tea bags

Coffee
Instant drink mix
Cocoa
Gelatin mix
Pudding mix
Cake mix
Popcorn
Tomato sauce
Onions
Peanut butter
Mustard
Catsup
Mayonnaise
Shortening
Yeast
Spices
Multi vitamins

Long Term Supplies

Pressure canner and accessories
Canning book
Canning jars (10 cases per person)
Extra jar lids or reusable lids w/extra gaskets
Vegetable seeds
Garden tools
Fuel barrels w/ hand pump (2 - 55 gal. drums)
Fuel
Fuel stabilizer
Aspirin

Ibuprofen
Antibiotic ointment
Band-Aids & gauze
Burn cream
Iodine
Rubbing alcohol
Hydrogen peroxide
Epsom salt
Dental floss
Eye drops
Antacid tablets
Pepto Bismol
Surgical tape
Butterfly closures
Calamine lotion
5 gal. Storage buckets w/ lids
Hand operated grain mill
Hand operated meat grinder
Bicycle
2 way radios
Solar panels
Wind turbine
Battery charger
Rechargeable batteries
LED lights

Household Supplies

Toilet paper
Soap

Feminine hygiene products
Disposable razors
Shaving cream
Hair trimming kit
Laundry detergent
Dish soap
Tooth paste
Shampoo
Pine oil cleaner
Unscented bleach
Freezer bags
Light bulbs
Paper towels
Trash bags
Pot scrubbers
Sponges
Baby powder
Hand lotion
Aluminum foil
Wax paper
Food wrap

Good to Have Items

Woodstove
Chain saw & splitting maul
Power inverter 1,500w+
Generator
Batteries 12v deep cycle
Candles or oil lamps & oil

Ammo
Shotgun
Work boots
Durable clothing
Duct Tape
Plastic sheathing
Carpentry tools

Barter Items

Sewing kits
Safety pins
Cloth diapers
Disposable lighters
Matches
Rubber tube repair kits
Lamp wicks
Lamp mantles
Candles
Dry bleach
Playing cards
Pencils
Writing pads
Aspirin
Antibiotics
Clothes pins
Duct tape
Plastic 3mil+
J B weld
Super glue

Velcro strips
Canning lids
Seeds
Gardening tools
Fishing supplies
Soap
Clothing
Fuel
Fuel stabilizer
Liquor
Ammo
Tobacco products
Chocolate

Business Opportunities

Auto repair
Tire repair
Roadside service
Fruit and vegetable stand
Poultry and egg sales
DVD rentals
Small country store
Milled grains
Bakery
Small engine repair
Lawn maintenance and snow removal
Welding
Honey sales
Livestock production and sales

Diner that serves homegrown food
Furniture reupholsters
Furniture construction and repair
Electronics repair
Appliance repair
Carpentry
Masonry
Plumbing
Electrician
Painter
Metal fabrication
Livestock butchering service
Tree removal and trimming
Auto body repair
Boat construction and maintenance
Winery
Casket construction
Monument service
Cabinet maker
Clothing repair and sewing services
Barber shop/beauty salon
Bed and breakfast inn
Campground
RV Park
Portable lumber mill service
Desktop publishing

Internet Resources

www.apmex.com	Precious metals
www.beprepared.com	Emergency supplies
www.bulkfoods.com	Bulk foods
www.foodsaver.com	Vacuum sealers
www.reusablecanninglids.com	Tattler canning lids
www.zappworks.com	Nickel Iron batteries
www.mcmurrayhatchery.com	Poultry and supplies
www.mountainvalleygrowers.com	Herb plants
www.southernexposure.com	Organic seeds
www.enasco.com	Farm & ranch supplies
www.lehmans.com	Nonelectric supplies
www.hoeggergoatsupply.com	Goat supplies
www.sunelectric.com	Solar products
www.stanpacnet.com	Milk bottles
www.vetamerica.com	Vet supplies
www.spillehoney.com	Honey bees
www.brushymountainbeefarm.com	Bee supplies
www.survivinghealthy.com	Medical preparedness
www.midwayusa.com	Shooting supplies
www.cabelas.com	Shooting supplies
www.gunpartscorp.com	Gun repair parts
www.e-sarcoinc.com	Gun repair parts
www.backwoodshome.com	Country living mag
www.motherearthnews.com	Country living mag
www.wnd.com	News site
www.lewrockwell.com	Economics
www.shadowstats.com	Economic analysis
www.theinternationalforecaster.com	Economics
www.build-a-gassifier.com	Producer gas plans

Reading List

The Have-More Plan
The Alpha Strategy
Barnyard in your Backyard
Root Cellaring
Grow it
The Backyard Orchardist
Small Scale Grain Raising
Brown's Alcohol Motor fuel Cookbook
Ditch Medicine
Ball Complete Book of Home Preserving
5000 Year Leap
Human Action

ABOUT THE AUTHOR

T R Chatham is a combat veteran and small business owner who grew up on the Chesapeake Bay.